The Best Torquay United Football Chants Ever …

The Best Torquay United Football Chants Ever ...

The Best
Torquay United
Football Chants Ever ...

and also the rudest

A Fan

The Best Torquay United Football Chants Ever ...

Unofficial and Unauthorised

All the chants in this book are common chants sung on the terrace during football matches, and are written here in a light hearted way they are not the thoughts and views of the authors.

Copyright © InterviewBooks.com
All rights reserved,
including the right of reproduction
in whole or in part in any form.

ISBN 978-0-557-19106-2

Designed and written by A Fan

To all the Gulls fans out there, sing up for the lads!

The Best Torquay United Football Chants Ever ...

Contents

Introduction	. . . . .	9
1. Classic Chants	. . . .	11
2. Torquay Heroes Songs	. .	17
3. Give them some stick	. .	23
4. The referees a w*nker	. .	35
5. The Best Torquay Websites	. .	39
6. Torquay Supporters Clubs	. .	43
7. The Best of the Rest	. . .	47

The Best Torquay United Football Chants Ever ...

Introduction

Thank you for taking the time to read "The Best Torquay United Football Chants Ever …". In this book we take a light hearted look at the popular chants, sung from the terrace each week.

Most of the chants sung from the terrace are sung in a light hearted way but are sung to provoke the players or fans from the other team.

This book covers all of the popular songs; no chant has been kept out of this book for being politically incorrect or too rude.

Get ready to have a laugh at the other teams' expense …

The Best Torquay United Football Chants Ever ...

Chapter 1

Classic Chants

The Best Torquay United Football Chants Ever ...

Chapter 1   -   Classic Chants

Stand up
If you love Torquay
Stand up
If you love Torquay

And its Torquay United
Torquay United F.C.
We're by far the greatest team,
The world has ever seen ...
(repeat)

Oh when the Gulls
(Oh when the Gulls),
Go marching in,
(Go marching in),
Oh when the Gulls go marching in,
I want to be in that number,
Oh when the Gulls go marching in ...

Who's that team they call Torquay
Who's that team we all adore?
They're the boys in yellow and white,
And we're f**king dynamite,

Yellow Army,
Yellow Army,
Yellow Army,
Yellow Army,

We are Torquay
We are Torquay
We are Torquay
We are Torquay
We are Torquay

We love you Torquay.
We do,
We love you Torquay
We do,
We love you Torquay
We do,
Oh Torquay we love you

The Best Torquay United Football Chants Ever ...

E I, E I, E I, O,
Up the league we go,
When we win promotion,
This is what we'll sing,

We are Torquay
We are Torquay
Buckle is our king ...

Torquay till I die,
I'm Torquay till I die,
I know I am,
I'm sure I am,
I'm Torquay till I die

Come on Torquay
Come on Torquay
Come on Torquay
Come on Torquay ...

(clap, clap, clap, clap, clap, clap clap)
Torquay
(clap, clap, clap, clap, clap, clap clap)
Torquay
(clap, clap, clap, clap, clap, clap clap)
Torquay

Come on you yellows
Come on you yellows
Come on you yellows
Come on you yellows

Stand up if your one nil up,
Stand up if your one nil up,
Stand up if your one nil up,
Stand up if your one nil up ...

Hello, Hello. We are the Torquay Boys
Hello, Hello. We are the Torquay Boys
And if you are a Exeter fan,
Surrender or you die,
We all follow Torquay ...

Chapter 2

Torquay United Heroes Songs

The Best Torquay United Football Chants Ever ...

Chapter 2 - Torquay United Heroes Songs

Lee, Lee, Lee Mansell
Lee, Lee, Lee Mansell
Lee, Lee, Lee Mansell

We got the boy from up the road, Benyon Benyon
We got the boy from up the road, Benyon Benyon
We got the boy from up the road

He gets the ball he scores a goal
Elliot Benyon Torquays number 9

Paul Buckles yellow army (clap, clap, clap, clap)
Paul Buckles yellow army (clap, clap, clap, clap)

He's here
He's there
He's every f*ckin where
Kevin Hill
Kevin Hill

The Best Torquay United Football Chants Ever ...

Stevie Woods my lord
Stevie Woods
Stevie Woods my lord
Stevie Woods

Feed the Sills,
Feed the Sills,
Feed the Sills and he will score

There's only one Wayne Carlisle
One Wayne Carlisle
He used to be sh*te but now he's alright
Walking in a Carlisle wonderland

Super, super Scott,
Super, super Scott,
Super, super Scott,
Super Scotty Rendell

The Best Torquay United Football Chants Ever ...

Oh Chris Hargreaves
You are the Love Of My Life
Oh Chris Hargreaves
I'd let you Shag my Wife
Oh Chris Hargreaves
I Want Long Hair Too

The Best Torquay United Football Chants Ever …

Chapter 3

Give them some stick

The Best Torquay United Football Chants Ever ...

Chapter 3 - *Give them some stick*

Oh Exeter
Oh Exeter
Is full of s*it
Is full of s*it
Oh Exeter is full of s*it, its full of s*it, s*it and more s*it
Oh Exeter is full of s*it

Can you hear Exeter sing? No, no

Can you hear Exeter sing? No, no

Can you hear Exeter sing?

I can't hear a f*cking thing,

Woah woah woah

If you all hate Exeter clap your hands
If you all hate Exeter clap your hands
If you all hate Exeter
If you all hate Exeter
If you all hate Exeter clap your hands ...

When I was just a little boy,
I asked my mother what should I be,
Should I be Torquay or should I be Exeter
Here's what she said to me,
Wash your mouth out son,
And fetch your fathers gun,
And shoot the Exeter scum,
And shoot the Exeter scum,
We hate Exeter we hate Exeter ...

We forgot that,
We forgot that,
We forgot that you were here
We forgot that you were here ...

S*it ground no fans,
S*it ground no fans,
S*it ground no fans,
S*it ground no fans ...

You're supposed to,
You're supposed to,
You're supposed to be at home,
You're supposed to be at home ...

Sit down, shut up,
Sit down, shut up,
Sit down, shut up,
Sit down, shut up,
Sit down, shut up,
Sit down, shut up ...

Away in a manger,
No crib for his bed,
The little Lord Jesus laid down and he said:

We hate Exeter

We hate Exeter

Premiership,
Yer havin' a laugh,
Premiership,
Yer havin' a laugh,
Premiership,
Yer havin' a laugh,
Premiership,
Yer havin' a laugh,
Premiership,
Yer havin' a laugh ...

Shall we sing a,
Shall we sing a,
Shall we sing a song for you,
Shall we sing a song for you …

We had joy,
We had fun,
We had Exeter on the run,
But the fun didn't last coz the f**kers ran to fast ...

Hark now hear,
The Torquay Sing,
Exeter ran away,
And we will fight for ever more,
Because of Derby Day ...

You are a farmer,
A dirty farmer,
Your only happy when making hay,
Your mums an info,
Your dads a scarecrow ,
So please don't take my tractor away

Are you Exeter
Are you Exeter
Are you Exeter in disguise,
Are you Exeter in disguise ...

Your sister is your mother,
Your father is your brother,
Your f*ckin one another,
The Exeter family

Your ground's too big for you,
Your ground's too big for you,
Your ground's too big for you,

Build a bonfire,
Build a bonfire,
Put Exeter on the top,
Put Plymouth in the middle,
And we'll burn the f*cking lot!

They're here,
They're there,
They're every f*cking where,
Empty seats, empty seats ...

F*ck all,

You've never won f*ck all

You've never won f*ck all

You've never won f*ck all

F*ck all,

You've never won f*ck all

Jingle bells,

Jingle bells

Jingle all the way

Oh what fun it is to see Torquay win away

Hey!

(Tune: Jingle Bells)

Stand up if you hate Exeter
Stand up if you hate Exeter
Stand up if you hate Exeter

Sit down if you hate Exeter
Sit down if you hate Exeter
Sit down if you hate Exeter

Dance round if you hate Exeter
Dance round if you hate Exeter
Dance round if you hate Exeter

Who, Who, Who, Who ...

(Sung when the other team makes a substitution and the players name is announced)

Dream on, Dream on,
With envy in your heart,
And you'll never with the league,
You'll never win the league - again, again, again ...

You are a scouser, an ugly scouser,
You're only happy on giro day,
Your mum's out thieving,
Your dad's drug dealing,
But please don't take my hubcaps away ...

Steve Gerrard, Gerrard,
He kisses the badge on his chest,
Then puts in a transfer request,
Steve Gerrard, Gerrard ...

You scouse b***ards,
You scouse b***ards,
You scouse b***ards ...

Are you watching?
Are you watching?
Are you watching Exeter
Are you watching Exeter

If you hate Plymouth clap your hands,
If you hate Plymouth clap your hands,
If you hate Plymouth
If you hate Plymouth
If you hate Plymouth
Clap your hands ...

Glory Hunters Man United!

Glory Hunters Man Untied!

Glory Hunters Man United!

Support Your Local Team!

Feed the scousers,
Let them know it's Christmas time ...

The Best Torquay United Football Chants Ever ...

Chapter 4

The referees a w*nker

The Best Torquay United Football Chants Ever ...

Chapter 4 - *The referees a w*nker*

The referees a w*nker
The referees a w*nker
The referees a w*nker

Where's your Father?
Where's your Father?
Where's your Father, referee
you ain't got one
your a B*st*rd
your a B*st*rd referee

12 men ...
You've only got 12 men ...
You've only got 12 men ...

12 men ...
You've only got 12 men ...
You've only got 12 men ...

The Best Torquay United Football Chants Ever ...

Chapter 5

The Best Torquay United Websites

The Best Torquay United Football Chants Ever ...

Chapter 5 - The Best Torquay United Websites

Official Web Site

www.torquayunited.com

Unofficial Web Sites

www.barnstaplegulls.co.uk

www.TorquayUnited.net

www.torquayfansforum.proboards.com/index.cgi

www.torquayfans.com

www.torquayunited-mad.co.uk

The Best Torquay United Football Chants Ever ...

Chapter 6

Torquay United Supporters Clubs

The Best Torquay United Football Chants Ever ...

Chapter 6 - Torquay United Supporters Clubs

Supporters Club

www.torquaysupporters.com

Gloucester Gulls

www.gloucestergulls.co.uk

North Devon Gulls

www.barnstaplegulls.co.uk

The Best Torquay United Football Chants Ever ...

Chapter 7

The Best of The Rest

The Best Torquay United Football Chants Ever ...

Chapter 7 - The Best of the Rest

Some of the best ever football chants from other teams.

"You're just a poor man's Evian, you're just a poor man's Evian"
Sung in the lower leagues to Buxton FC

"You're just a fat Eddie Murphy"
Sung about Jimmy Floyd Hasselbaink

You're not yodelling, You're not yodelling any more"
Sung when playing in Europe when playing any Swiss team

"We hate Tuesday, hate Tuesday"
Sung in response to Sheffield United's chant of "We hate Wednesday"

"You should've stayed on the telly"
Sung to Shearer during his brief reign as manager of Newcastle

The Best Torquay United Football Chants Ever ...

"Sit down Pinocchio, sit down Pinocchio"
Sung to Liverpool's Phil Thompson

"You've got Di Canio, we've got your stereo"
Liverpool fans in response to West Ham's chant of "We've got Di Canio"

"Two Andy Gorams, there's only two Andy Gorams"
Celtic fans to Andy Goram after it was revealed the keeper was diagnosed with schizophrenia

"It's just like watching The Bill"
Sung when police come onto the pitch to the tune of "it's just like watching Brazil"

"Nani are you OK? Are you OK Nani"
Manchester United fans towards Michael Jackson look a like Nani to the tune of smooth criminal

The Best Torquay United Football Chants Ever ...

We would like to thank everyone that has taken part in the book, and all those that have submitted material and features for the book.

The Best Torquay United Football Chants Ever ...

The Best Torquay United Football Chants Ever ...

The Best Torquay United Football Chants Ever ...

Printed in Great Britain
by Amazon.co.uk, Ltd.,
Marston Gate.